Inside the Zoo Nursery

INSIDE THE ZOO NURSERY

Roland Smith

PHOTOGRAPHS BY WILLIAM MUÑOZ

COBBLEHILL BOOKS

Dutton   New York

To Jonolyn McCusker and all of the step-creatures
she has helped over the years

ACKNOWLEDGMENTS

The author and photographer wish to thank the following organizations for their help with this book: Arizona-Sonora Desert Museum, Brookfield Zoo, Busch Gardens, Cincinnati Zoo, Fossil Rim Wildlife Center, Lincoln Park Zoo, Los Angeles Zoo, Lowry Park Zoo, Point Defiance Zoo & Aquarium, Sea World of Florida, St. Louis Zoo, Rio Grande Zoo, and the Woodland Park Zoo.

Numerous people assisted with this book. To list them individually would comprise a book in itself. We would like to send a special thanks to John and Janice Houck, Mike Jones DVM, Will Waddell, and Byron Olsen for reviewing the manuscript. We are also grateful to Dorothy Hinshaw Patent for her editorial comments and for being a good friend.

Library of Congress Cataloging-in-Publication Data

Smith, Roland, date.
 Inside the zoo nursery / Roland Smith ; photographs by William Muñoz.
  p. cm.
 Includes index.
 Summary: Explains the different reasons why some zoo animal babies are raised in the zoo nursery and examines what happens to them when they get there and after they leave.
 ISBN 0-525-65084-9
 1. Zoo nurseries—Juvenile literature. 2. Zoo animals—Infancy—Juvenile literature.
[1. Zoo nurseries. 2. Zoo animals. 3. Animals—Infancy.] I. Muñoz, William, ill.
II. Title.
SF408.S65 1993   636.088'9—dc20   92-3344   CIP   AC

Published in the United States of America by Cobblehill Books, an affiliate of Dutton Children's Books, a division of Penguin Books USA Inc., 375 Hudson Street, New York, New York 10014

Designed by Charlotte Staub Printed in Hong Kong First Edition 10 9 8 7 6 5 4 3 2 1

CONTENTS

A nursery keeper holds a baboon that is ready to go back with the troop.

Chapter One

✦

ZOO ORPHANS

It is three o'clock in the morning and David Hansen is tired. He has been sitting outside of the baboon exhibit since five o'clock the previous evening. David is the primate keeper at the zoo — the man who takes care of the monkeys and apes. He is watching a female who is about to give birth to her first baby. At 3:15 the infant baboon is born. The baby appears healthy — its movements strong. David watches intently as the mother begins to clean the baby. The other members of the baboon troop tentatively approach the mother for a closer look at the infant. The mother bares her long canine teeth at them, warning them not to get too close. Most of the troop heed her warning and keep their distance. But the lead female disregards her threat.

1

Instead of backing away like the others, she rushes in and snatches the baby from the mother, then retreats to the highest point of the cage, with the baby dangling by one arm. The new mother chases the baby thief. Around and around the exhibit they go. But, weak from giving birth, the new mother quickly tires. Eventually she gives up, and the two females sit in opposite corners of the exhibit ignoring each other.

David had spent most of the night watching the mother baboon because she was new to the troop, and this being her first baby, he suspected that there might be problems. But he didn't plan on the dominant female stealing the baby. He tells himself to stay calm, knowing that panic will not help the baby. The wrong action on his part could worsen an already dangerous situation. He has to be very careful. The exhibit is twenty feet tall, and if the female drops the baby from this height, it could be killed. He decides that his only hope of rescuing the baby is to coax the baboons into the off-exhibit holding area.

In the primate kitchen he fills a bucket with fresh fruits and vegetables to entice the baboons into the holding area. The holding area is used to contain the baboons while the keeper is cleaning their exhibit. It consists of a series of small cages connected by sliding doors. As the baboons move through the series of cages David can open and close the sliding doors to isolate the animals into separate cages. With the female and the baby in a small cage, the risk of injury from a fall is less, and David will have a better chance of taking the baby from the female and returning it to its real mother.

Before going to the holding area, David calls his supervisor, the animal curator, and tells her what has happened. She tells him that she will call the veterinarian. David suggests that she also contact the zoo nursery keeper, in case the baby has to be taken there for hand-rearing.

David goes to the back of the baboon exhibit and puts the food in the holding area. Then he opens all of the sliding doors. The baboons are reluctant to come in, even for food. They are not used to coming into the holding area at

A young baboon grooms her sister.

four in the morning. David waits patiently. After several minutes, the big male baboon sticks his head through the door and peers suspiciously into the holding area. He sees and smells the fresh fruits and vegetables, then extends his long gray arm and tries to grab a piece of food. Anticipating this, David laid the food just out of a baboon's reach.

After awhile the male slowly inches his body into the holding area. When he is inside David shuts a separation door before the animal can dash back out. He then shifts the male to the farthest holding cage.

3

David baits the holding area again. The next baboon to come in is the dominant female, dragging the baby behind her. The baby looks very weak, but at least now it is inside the holding area so it can't be injured from a long fall. Once inside, the baboon begins to eat and lets go of the baby. David manages to shift her down one cage, separating her from the baby. Then he opens the holding cage and retrieves the infant. It has a few scrapes and is cold, but otherwise seems all right. He gently wraps the baby in his coat and sets it to the side. Now he has to catch the mother.

There are three baboons remaining. David keeps baiting the holding area. The last baboon to come in is the baby's mother. Securing the doors, David picks the baby up and holds it close to his body to warm it. He looks at his watch. It has taken nearly an hour to get the baboons into the holding area and separated.

David heads back to the primate kitchen, where the zoo's veterinarian is waiting for him. Unwrapping the baby from David's jacket, the veterinarian examines it.

"It's a girl," he says. "Slightly chilled, and weak from the ordeal, but other than that she looks healthy enough."

Just then, the animal curator and the nursery keeper arrive.

They too examine the baby. Carla, the nursery keeper, offers her little finger to the baby, and weakly, the baby starts to suck on it.

"Good sucking reflex, considering the circumstances."

"Does the mother have milk?"

"Looks like it," David says.

"What do you think we ought to do?"

"The baboons are locked in the holding area," David explains. "I can put them all back into the exhibit except for the mother. She might take care of the baby if she's alone."

"It's worth a try."

Before putting the baby in with the mother, David lets the other baboons back out into the exhibit. He wants the introduction to be as calm as possible. He places the baby in the adjoining holding cage, then opens the door between, giving the female access to her youngster. With this done David and the others stand at a distance and watch.

The mother tentatively approaches the baby. She bends down and sniffs, then touches it. The baby squeals. Startled by the sound, she jumps back and retreats to the far corner of the cage. After a few moments the baby quiets down, but the mother remains in the corner, her attention focused away from the baby.

"I don't like the way this looks," the veterinarian says. "We'll give it some more time though," he adds.

They watch for a half hour longer, hoping that the female will pick up her

Whenever possible animals are reared in a group as are these Thompson's gazelle calves.

baby and start taking care of it. But nothing changes — the mother continues to ignore her baby.

"I'm afraid it's getting chilled again," David says. "I think we'd better take her to the nursery."

Reluctantly, they all agree.

David separates the mother from her baby by shifting her down one cage. He then takes the tiny baboon out of the holding area and wraps her in his jacket again and carefully hands the bundle to Carla.

"What shall we call her?" Carla asks.

David thinks a moment. "How about Mandy?"

"Okay, Mandy," Carla says looking into the infant's wrinkled face. "Let's see what we can do about finding you a home in the nursery."

NATURAL MOTHERS MAKE THE BEST MOTHERS

People who work at zoos know that hand-rearing a baby animal is a poor substitute for a mother's care. But there are times when taking an infant from its natural mother cannot be avoided.

Young animals are sometimes removed for hand-rearing because they have been hurt, or there is the threat of injury from others in the exhibit. A baby's mother might be injured or die, leaving an orphan whose only chance of survival is to be hand-reared.

Endangered animals are sometimes hand-reared because they are so rare. If the zoo personnel don't believe that the female can raise the baby on her own, it may be taken to the nursery.

Sometimes a mother will have too many offspring to care for properly. For instance, twins can be very difficult for primates to raise because they carry their youngsters wherever they go. Sometimes a mother doesn't have enough milk to raise a single baby, and therefore it has to be hand-reared.

An infant might be taken from its mother to be raised with other hand-reared babies of like kind in the nursery. Whenever possible, zoos like to raise primates with primates, cats with cats, and hoofed animals with hoofed animals so they can learn from one another.

WHEN TO HAND-REAR

Regardless of the reason for taking a baby from its natural mother, the decision to hand-rear is difficult. These questions might be asked before taking a baby from its mother:

- What is the condition and behavior of the newborn, its mother, its father, and the others occupying the exhibit?
- Will the other animals in the exhibit leave the mother and infant alone?
- Does the zoo have the proper facilities and the trained staff to raise this baby?
- Are there enough staff members to feed the youngster during the night shift?
- How rare is this newborn?
- If left with its natural mother, what are the chances of it surviving?
- Has this type of baby been hand-reared before? Were these attempts successful?
- What will hand-rearing do to the infant's natural development? Will it be able to adjust to a life with its own kind after being raised by humans?

Only after such questions have been answered in a positive way, is the decision made to take a baby from its natural mother.

When not feeding or holding babies, nursery keepers observe them and keep careful records.

Chapter Two

INSIDE THE ZOO NURSERY

With Mandy wrapped snugly in David's jacket, Carla walks briskly from the primate house to the zoo nursery. On the way she thinks of all the steps necessary to keep Mandy alive. The veterinarian said that he would meet her at the nursery after stopping at the zoo hospital to pick up some supplies.

When Carla gets to the nursery, she turns on the lights and is greeted by a loud bellow from the dromedary camel calf, Clark.

"Sorry to wake you so early," Carla says and rubs him on the head. Clark had been at the zoo nursery for several months. He is getting big and it wouldn't be long before he outgrew his nursery pen. Soon they would take Clark to the

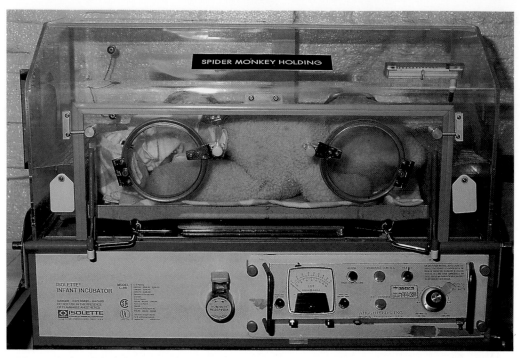

Human infant incubators are often used for zoo babies because the temperature can be controlled, and nursery staff can see the babies easily.

camel yard to live with the other camels in the zoo's collection. She would miss him.

Carla switches on the empty human/infant incubator. It would take awhile for the incubator to reach the 85 degree temperature required for newborn primates; until then, Carla will keep Mandy wrapped up in the jacket to keep her warm.

For the time being they would keep Mandy by herself in an incubator. Eventually she would be put in with the baby spider monkey that had arrived at the nursery two weeks earlier. As cage companions, the two primates could play with each other and keep each other company. Carla feels badly about Mandy's mother rejecting her, but Mandy's presence in the nursery would help the young spider monkey, and the spider monkey would help Mandy.

Carla takes a clipboard from the wall and starts a record on Mandy, writing down the time and date of Mandy's birth and the circumstances behind her coming to the zoo nursery. Before Mandy left there would be page after page of notes regarding her progress and care. This valuable hand-rearing information is shared with other zoo nurseries so that they can learn from the experience of others.

The zoo's veterinarian walks into the nursery carrying his medical bag.

"Let's see how our patient is doing," he says.

Carefully, Carla unwraps Mandy from the jacket and lays her on the table. The bright lights of the nursery and sudden loss of security and warmth scare Mandy and she lets out a loud whoop of protest.

"Nothing wrong with her vocal cords," the veterinarian says. Some of the other orphaned primates that he has examined at the zoo nursery were too weak to protest. It was the silent baby primates that worried him most. He takes the stethoscope out of his bag.

"Why don't you take her temperature while I listen to her heart and lungs."

The heartbeat is strong and regular, and the lungs sound clear of any congestion.

"Everything sounds good. What about the temperature?"

Carla checks the thermometer. "Ninety-eight on the button."

"Well, I'd say that she's in pretty good shape," the veterinarian says. "Let's weigh her and draw some blood."

The veterinarian draws a small amount of blood which he will send to the laboratory to be analyzed to see if there is any infection that will have to be treated. After he is finished Carla weighs the youngster and writes the weight on the chart. From now on Mandy will be weighed every day to keep track of how she is growing.

11

"I guess that's all I can do for her tonight," the veterinarian says. "Let's put her in the incubator and see what we can do about getting her something to eat."

SURROGATE MOTHERS

A "surrogate mother" takes the place of the natural mother in raising an infant. In a zoo nursery, humans serve as surrogate mothers for a great variety of young animals. Because of the amount of time spent in caring for these youngsters, the babies brought to the zoo nursery usually end up with several "mothers." It takes a special kind of skill to work with orphaned animals.

Most of the babies that arrive in the zoo nursery are very delicate, and many die because of their frail conditions. Nursery workers must not only be skilled animal handlers with amazing patience, they also must be able to tolerate the stress and disappointment of losing an animal that they have grown fond of.

ENCLOSURE DESIGN

Every baby animal has different housing needs. The zoo nursery must be able to accommodate animals as big as a 200-pound elephant calf, to a kangaroo rat weighing less than an ounce at birth.

Human infant incubators are often used for newborn primates, small mammals, and birds. Incubators are ideal because the temperature and humidity can be controlled, and the baby can be observed without having to open the cage.

Young hoofed animals are put in pens. The floors are covered with wood shavings or straw to give the animals better footing and a soft place to lay down.

Flexibility is the primary factor in designing enclosures for zoo babies.

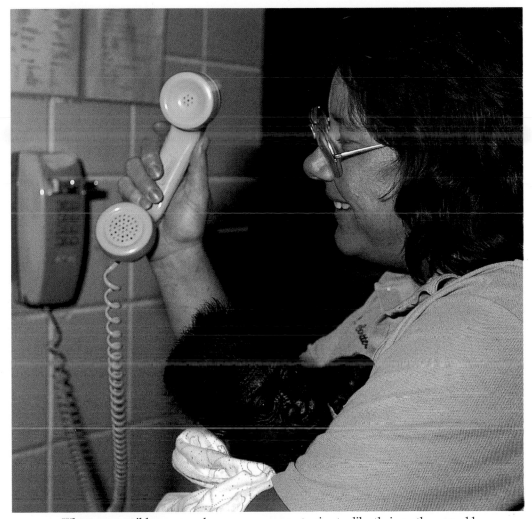
Whenever possible, nursery keepers carry young primates like their mothers would.

Because the nursery staff does not know what their next occupant is going to be, nursery enclosures are designed so they can be changed to house a wide variety of animals.

Besides fulfilling the environmental needs of the various infants, nursery enclosures also need to be "babyproof." This is especially true for primates. As

13

A nursery keeper feeds a very young kangaroo rat.

A nursery keeper hand feeds hay to a young muntjac.

14

These two clouded leopard cubs are just about old enough to go into the main zoo.

15

monkeys and apes grow older, not only can they crawl, climb, and jump, they can also unscrew, unhook, and undo almost anything that they can get their small but powerful fingers on.

As the babies grow older and become more active, they are moved into bigger enclosures more suited to their physical and psychological needs.

ZOO NURSERY SANITATION

Everything in the zoo nursery is kept immaculately clean. When coming into the nursery from outside, volunteers and staff step into a special footbath filled with disinfectant. The disinfectant kills germs and bacteria that could be harmful to the newborns. In some zoo nurseries volunteers and staff members have shoes that are worn only inside the nursery to prevent germs coming in from the outside.

Cages are disinfected to control bacteria that can harm baby animals.

All enclosures are cleaned and disinfected at least once a day, and antiseptic soap is used by all nursery workers before and after they pick up or handle each baby. In this way, germs are not passed to the other babies in the nursery.

Baby animals are susceptible to disease, especially the very young. Most critical among these are the baby primates because they are vulnerable to the same diseases that we are. Most zoo nurseries have a rule that if you are sick with a cold, the flu, or any other virus, you must stay away until you are better. If a nursery worker suspects that he or she might be coming down with something, the worker will wear a disposable mask when handling babies that are susceptible to human diseases to avoid the possible transfer of germs.

LEARNING WHOM TO TRUST

Unlike some domestic animals, wild animals have well-developed defense behaviors (like running or charging) that they use when frightened. This is called the "flight or fight response." This flight or fight behavior is especially well developed in baby animals that have been with their natural mother for a time before being removed for hand-rearing. They have learned when to be afraid.

When faced with danger, animals like antelope and deer fawns, will run away (take "flight") from the danger. Other animals, such as elephant calves, might charge ("fight") when frightened.

The nursery staff must be very careful when handling animals in order to avoid injury to the animals and themselves. If the baby animal might run or charge, the keepers will put the animal in a pen or cage where it will feel secure. To add to the animal's sense of security, visual barriers can be used to block out the animal's view of people. The light in the pen might be dimmed, because bright lights often frighten animals. When working around nervous animals,

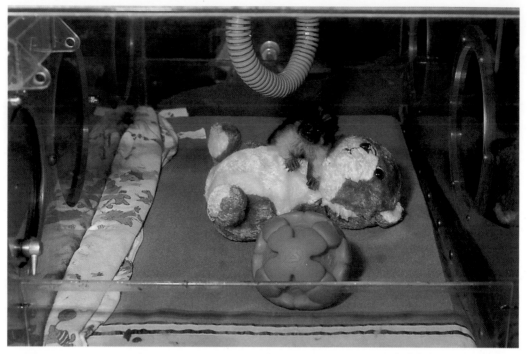

Many baby animals cling to their mothers for the first few months of life. Stuffed animals are sometimes used as a substitute for babies to cling to.

nursery staff will keep their voices very low. Sometimes, to get the animals accustomed to sounds that they are likely to encounter in their new environment, a radio will be played very quietly near their enclosure.

Usually, after a few days a frightened animal will begin to get used to its new environment, and develop a trust for its new mothers. When this happens, the nursery keepers can move around more freely when they are near the animal.

IMPRINTING

As with humans, social contact is very important to the psychological development of animals.

18

A mother giraffe leans down to check her calf.

Hoofed animals of different types can be kept together in a group situation. Primates of the same size can be kept together, as can cats of the same size. Of course, this is not always possible because companion animals are not available. And sometimes, even if companion animals are available, it doesn't always work because animals don't always get along with each other.

If a suitable cage mate is not available, the nursery staff must provide all the social contact that is necessary for the infant's development.

When babies are born they "imprint" on their natural mothers. The mother becomes the baby's security. By watching her, the baby learns the rules of survival. Imprinting is one way that a llama learns that it is a llama, and a

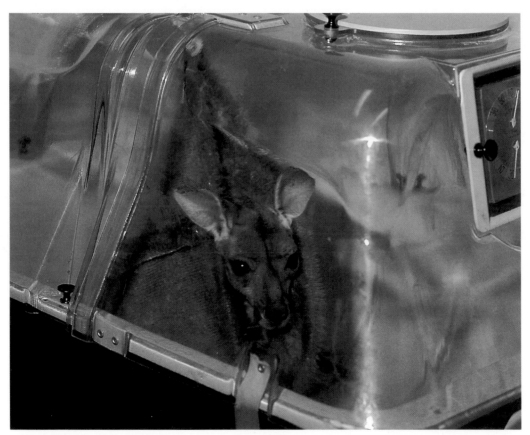

An artificial pouch was made for this young wallaby. If it was with its mother it would stay in the pouch for many months.

20

chimpanzee learns that it is a chimpanzee. It helps the youngster grow into a psychologically healthy adult that will fit in well with animals of its own kind.

When an animal baby has to be taken from its mother at a young age and raised by humans, the infant may imprint on humans. As the youngster matures, this can cause problems, especially when the time comes for it to be introduced to animals of its own kind. Every type of animal species (including the human animal) has different rules by which it lives. These rules are usually learned when very young, and the transition from one set of rules to another can be difficult.

To understand this, imagine for a moment that you were adopted by a group of gorillas when you were a baby. For the first years of your life you were carried through the forest by your surrogate gorilla mother. You slept outside, you played gorilla games, and you searched for food in the forest. Then when you were five years old you were taken away from the gorillas and put back with humans. In this new society you found that there was a spoken language, and that you were expected to wear clothes. Food was paid for at a grocery store, and this strange food was eaten with utensils. Instead of sleeping on the ground in the forest, you were made to sleep on a bed in a house. Almost everything would be different from what you were used to. It would take a long time to learn a new way of behaving.

In the zoo nursery, imprinting cannot be totally avoided, but its effects can be lessened by letting baby animals socialize with species of their own or similar kind. Another way to reduce the effects of imprinting is to put the baby back with its herd or group as soon as possible.

A siamang ape is isolated in a squeeze cage so that it will not be injured while it receives an injection.

Chapter Three

❧ ❖ ❧

HAND-REARING
ZOO BABIES

The veterinarian talks with David and asks him to keep Mandy's mother isolated in the holding area.

"I'd like to make sure that she is all right after the birth," the veterinarian says. "And, if possible I would like to tranquilize her and see if we can get some colostrum milk from her to mix in with Mandy's artificial formula." They both know how important colostrum could be to a newborn.

In order to get into the holding cages, the baboons have to pass through a removable cage called a "squeeze cage." A squeeze cage is a cage that has one wall that moves inward and squeezes the animal so that it can't move and injure itself while it is getting an injection.

23

David knows that it will be easy to get the female into the squeeze cage. The baboons are used to the squeeze cage because every day they have to pass through it to get into and out of the holding area.

One by one he opens the holding cage doors. Mandy's mother moves eagerly down the row of holding cages thinking that she is going out into the exhibit with the other members of the troop. But, when she goes into the squeeze cage, instead of letting her out into the exhibit, David quickly begins to crank the handle that moves the wall. The female struggles for a few seconds but soon gives up. When she is unable to move, the veterinarian gives her a tranquilizer injection, and David opens the wall of the cage to give her more room. Within a few minutes she is sedated and the keeper pulls her out of the cage.

The veterinarian gives her a quick physical examination.

"She looks good," he says. "But keep her in the holding area today where you can watch her closely. Let's see if we can get some colostrum milk from her for Mandy."

The veterinarian uses a modified syringe to pull milk from her teat. They are lucky; for a first-time mother she has quite a bit of colostrum milk. They are able to pull a little over a tablespoon of the valuable liquid from the female. Mixed with Mandy's artificial formula, the colostrum will last for several feedings.

The keeper puts Mandy's mother back into the holding area before she wakes up. The veterinarian takes the milk to the nursery.

Carla mixes a small amount of the colostrum with the artificial formula. Before offering the bottle to Mandy, she warms the formula and tests the temperature by dribbling a little of it on her wrist. The formula is made from Similac® (a human milk replacer) diluted with water.

Mandy is sleeping peacefully in the incubator when Carla picks her up

Milk is warmed before it is fed to the babies.

and wraps her in a soft towel. Mandy struggles for a time, but soon gives up. Cradling Mandy in her arms, the keeper gently squeezes the bottle so that some of the formula runs into Mandy's mouth. She then puts the nipple in Mandy's mouth, and Mandy begins to nurse eagerly.

Carla is relieved. Baby animals don't always like the artificial formula.

BABY MAMMALS

One factor separating mammals from other animals is that mammals suckle their young. In fact the word mammal is from the Latin word *mammalia*, which means breast. All mammals receive their first nourishment from their mother's milk. Some mammals, like shrews, are dependent on this milk for only a few days. Others, like elephants and gorillas, can be dependent on milk for several months or years.

25

MOTHER'S MILK

A mother's natural milk is the perfect food for her baby, and the design of her mammary gland is the perfect system for delivering this milk.

All milks are similar but the percentage of certain ingredients, such as fat, differs to suit the biological needs of the animal it is designed for. For instance, California sea lion milk contains a higher percentage of fat (35 percent) than other milks. The fat in the milk helps in building a blubber layer which keeps the young sea lion warm in the frigid water. Other mammal milks, like that from chimpanzees, have a lower percentage of fat (3.7 percent). This is because a baby chimp not only has hair to protect it from the cold, but its mother carries it for the first few years of its life, keeping the youngster warm with her own body heat.

Duplicating a mother's natural milk can be difficult, and the best the nursery staff can hope for is to come as close as possible. The baby itself is the best indication of whether the artificial milk is working. If the baby is gaining weight, appears strong, and its stool is normal, the nursery staff can assume that the replacement milk is doing an adequate job of nourishing the baby.

There are many commercial replacement milks available to feed to baby animals. Domestic cat, dog, pig, and horse milk replacers are a few of them. Besides these, there are several milks made for human infants. Many of these replacements can be used as a substitute for mother's milk. Baby carnivores, or meat-eaters, can be fed domestic kitten or puppy milk replacers. Baby bears have been successfully reared on kitten milk replacer. Apes and monkeys can be fed products used for human infants.

Zoo babies are sometimes fed milks from domestic animals like cows and goats. To make these milks more like their mother's natural milk, ingredients like egg yolks, high protein cereal, calcium, vitamins, and other ingredients are sometimes added.

Nothing can replace mother's milk.

COLOSTRUM

One essential ingredient contained in mother's milk not found in replacements is "colostrum." Colostrum is the first milk secreted from the mammary gland after a baby is born and is produced only for a short period. This milk contains antibodies that are necessary for the baby to fight off disease. Antibodies are special proteins in the blood that neutralize germs that can cause disease.

Colostrum is important because many newborns do not have functioning immune systems to protect them from disease. Instead they rely on their mothers' colostrum milk to protect them until their own immune systems are activated.

There are several ways of providing colostrum for newborn animals. The ideal way would be to get the colostrum milk directly from the mother, but

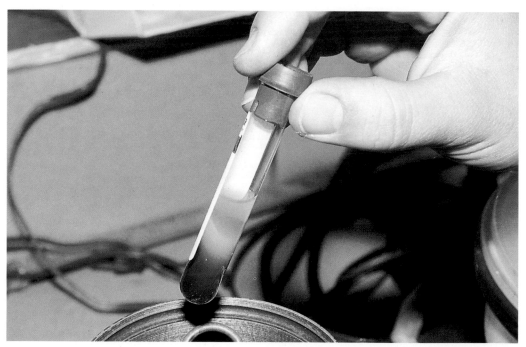

After spinning the blood, the clear serum separates. Photograph by Roland Smith.

because wild animals are not used to being milked, this is not always possible. Another way of providing colostrum to newborns is to feed them either goat or cow colostrum obtained from a local dairy. Dairies will often freeze colostrum for use in their own hand-reared babies. A colostrum substitute can also be made by drawing blood from an adult animal of the same species as the infant. The blood is put into a machine called a *centrifuge* that rapidly spins the blood until the red blood cells separate, forming a clear serum. This serum is fed to the infant and acts much like colostrum in providing antibodies to help fight off disease.

FEEDING BABY MAMMALS

When an infant has undergone its physical examination, and is adjusting to its new home in the nursery, attempts are made to feed it. Getting a baby animal to nurse is not always easy. Some youngsters that come into the nursery are very weak and do not have enough strength to suck milk from a nipple. Others might be strong, but they are fearful of the new way they are being handled, and therefore they refuse to nurse. Another reason for refusal to nurse is that some babies are taken from their mothers after they have been with them for a time. Because they have nursed from their natural mothers, they are not used to the taste of the artificial formula, or the feel of the artificial nipple.

It takes patience and gentle persistence to get some baby animals to nurse. If the infant is weak and doesn't have a "sucking reflex" the keeper may have to use an eyedropper or gently squeeze formula into the youngster's mouth until it has enough strength to suck formula from a nipple. At the other extreme there are baby animals that are very eager eaters. With animals like these, the keeper needs to be careful that the infant does not drink the formula too fast and inadvertently inhale it into its lungs. Another problem with youngsters that are

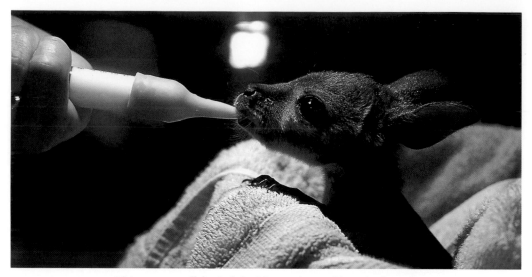

This young wallaby is fed with a syringe with a nipple on it.

eager eaters is that they eat so fast that air gets into the stomach. This can cause gas and discomfort, which can cause the baby to stop eating.

Keepers try to choose a nipple that is similar to the teat of the infant's natural mother. The size of the hole in the nipple depends on the consistency of formula. If the formula is thick the hole is big — if the formula is thin the hole is small.

While the babies nurse, keepers hold them like their mothers would. Animals not held by their mothers are allowed to orient themselves to the bottle as if it were the teat of their mother.

HOW MUCH FORMULA—HOW OFTEN?

If the infant were with its natural mother she would allow it to suckle often. In the zoo nursery each baby has to be put on a feeding schedule so that keepers can make sure that all the babies in the nursery get the attention that they need.

A young primate may be started on one ounce of formula every two hours. A baby rodent may be started on ⅕ teaspoon (or less) of formula as often as three times an hour.

The amount of food and the feeding frequency depend on the need of the particular animal. Generally, when a youngster is started on formula it is fed small amounts as often as every two hours. As the infant becomes stronger and begins to gain weight at a steady rate, it will be fed greater amounts at each feeding. These feedings may be spaced every three or four hours throughout the day.

The amount of formula taken at each feeding is carefully recorded on the animal's chart. In this way the keeper can detect any sudden drop in appetite, which might be an indication that the infant is ill.

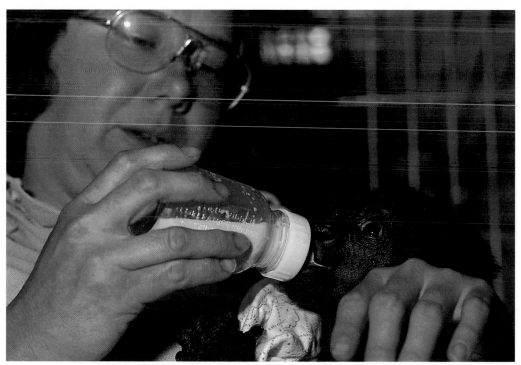

When feeding babies, nursery keepers hold the youngsters as their mothers would.

TUBE FEEDING

If coaxing a weakened baby to eat does not work, the infant may have to be fed with a stomach tube until it gains enough strength to be bottle fed.

Some orphaned babies, like porpoise and dolphin, are always fed with a stomach tube because there is not an artificial nipple that will allow them to nurse as they would from their natural mother.

Another reason for stomach-tube feeding is in cases where a baby is going to be reunited with its natural mother. Tube feeding is used to stabilize the baby

Orphaned porpoises are fed with a stomach tube. Photograph by Roland Smith.

quickly so it can be put back with its mother as soon as possible. If the baby got used to an artificial nipple, it might refuse to suckle on its natural mother.

To feed by this method a tube of the right diameter is gently inserted down the baby's throat. When the keeper is sure that the end of the tube is in the baby's stomach, a syringe is attached to the tube. Formula is then either poured into the syringe and allowed to "gravity flow" down the tube, or a plunger is used to gently push the formula into the stomach. Because stomach-tube feeding is involuntary, meaning that the baby cannot stop eating when it chooses, keepers are very careful about providing just the right amount of food.

PLAY

Most of us have seen puppies wrestle with each other or a kitten batting an object across the floor. By playing, mammals develop the physical and social skills that they will need in later life. Play is extremely important in the normal development of mammals.

Some zoo nurseries have special exercise/play areas for zoo babies.

Some baby mammals like kangaroos, cats, and primates are helpless at birth and totally dependent upon their mothers for survival. Mammals like these do not begin to play until they can move around on their own and their eyes are open. Other baby mammals, like elephants, deer, and giraffe, are born with their eyes open and the ability to move independently. Mammals like these are able to play within a few hours after birth.

In the zoo nursery animals are given constant opportunities to play. Keepers not only provide toys for them in their regular exhibits, but many nurseries have play areas that they can take the animals to for play sessions throughout the day.

If possible, compatible animals are put with each other and allowed to play. If compatible playmates are not available, the nursery staff will play with the baby.

HAND-REARING BABY BIRDS

Zoo nurseries receive many baby birds to raise because bird eggs in zoos are usually incubated artificially. As with mammals, some birds like parrots, crows, hawks, and owls are born totally dependent on their parents for survival. They are not able to leave their nests or feed themselves for several weeks. These dependent chicks are said to be *altricial* (al-trish-al), meaning they are helpless at hatching. Other birds, like ostriches, ducks, chickens, and pheasants, are able to eat and move independently as soon as they are out of the egg. Chicks like these are said to be *precocial* (pre-co-shal).

After hatching, a baby bird is usually left in the incubator for a few hours. This gives the chick a chance to recover from the ordeal of breaking out of the shell. At this point feeding is not important because the chick is still receiving nourishment from what is left of the *yolk sac* in the egg. When the baby bird has dried out and gained its strength back, it is taken to the nursery.

FEEDING ALTRICIAL CHICKS

Instead of getting nourishment from milk like mammals, the parents of altricial chicks feed them by either regurgitating soft food into their mouths, or feeding them small seeds, other plant material, or insects that have been mashed for easy ingestion.

In the zoo nursery altricial birds are fed soft food. The ingredients of this diet vary, depending on the species of bird and its nutritional requirements. The food is offered to the chicks with an eyedropper, tweezers, or put directly into their *crop* with a syringe. A crop is a special pouch in the bird's throat where food is stored or partially digested before being swallowed. Offering the chicks water is not usually necessary because they receive enough moisture from their diets.

Altricial chicks grow very rapidly and need to be fed as often as every two or three hours.

A keeper checks the eggs in the incubator. Most of the eggs laid at the zoo are artificially incubated. Photograph credit: Sea World.

Golden conure chicks are altricial when born. They grow quickly. When young they are kept in a nest made of towels inside an incubator.

This barn owl chick will stay in the incubator until it has regained its strength after hatching. Photograph by Jonolyn McCusker.

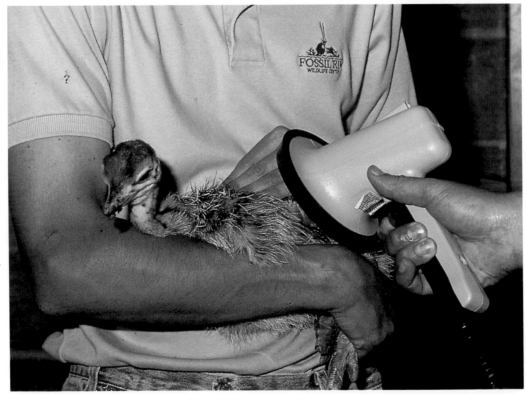

Ostrich chicks are precocial when born. They are able to follow their mother as soon as they hatch.

FEEDING PRECOCIAL CHICKS

When precocial chicks are taken from the incubator they are put in a *brooder*. A brooder replaces a mother in keeping the chicks warm. One type of brooder is designed with a wire floor so that droppings will fall through it and not soil the chicks. Another type of brooder has a solid floor covered with paper, which is changed often. Brooders are always kept clean to prevent bacteria from growing that could harm the fragile chicks.

Precocial chicks are not fed directly by their mothers. Instead, when they are strong enough to walk, they instinctively start pecking the ground in search of nourishment. In the zoo nursery this *pecking instinct* is used to get the chicks to eat. Small morsels of food are sprinkled in the brooder. As the chicks peck the ground they find the food and eat it.

TWENTY-FOUR HOURS A DAY

Many zoo babies need care twenty-four hours a day. At some zoos, depending on the number of babies, staff members may be assigned to the nursery after the zoo is closed. At other zoos the keepers who are responsible for caring for the zoo at night may go to the nursery and feed the babies. If it is thought to be in the best interest of the baby animal, a nursery staff member will take a baby animal home and care for it during the night. Some zoos do not have nurseries. When a baby has to be taken from its mother a staff member will adopt the baby and care for it until it is old enough to be on its own.

A baboon rides its mother piggyback.

Chapter Four

⌒ ✦ ⌒

LEAVING
THE ZOO NURSERY

Two weeks after Mandy came into the nursery she was put in with the young spider monkey. They shared the same incubator, and held each other when they slept. When they were old enough they were put in a larger enclosure. The two primates spent the day roughhousing, eating, and sleeping.

When Mandy was three months old, the nursery keepers started taking her to the primate house for visits. Eventually they began to reintroduce her to the baboon group. On these visits they put Mandy in the primate holding area. A screen separated her from the other baboons, but they could see and smell each other. At first Mandy was afraid of the baboons and wanted out of the holding area, but after a few visits she started to adjust to her future companions. The baboons came up to the screen and peered through the wire mesh. After several visits, the dominant female began to groom Mandy through the wire.

When Mandy was four months old, the nursery staff started to wean her. At nine months she was eating almost all solid food, and was fed only one bottle of formula a day.

After thirteen months in the zoo nursery, Mandy was totally weaned. It was time for her to move into the primate house permanently. At first she was kept in the holding area, separated from the other baboons by a screen.

One day the screen was opened and Mandy was allowed in with the others. The baboons were so used to her by this time that they paid little attention to her while she explored the exhibit. The keeper let her stay in the exhibit for about an hour. To get her back in the holding area he had to bait her with a bottle of formula. Each day the time she was allowed with the other baboons was increased.

During Mandy's time at the nursery her mother had another baby. This time there were no problems with the dominant female and she was able to rear it herself.

Eventually, Mandy was allowed to spend all day with the other baboons, and soon she became a permanent member of the troop.

How long a baby stays in the nursery depends on its needs. Eventually though, all of the animals outgrow the zoo nursery and are moved to more permanent homes. Some spend only a short time in the nursery, while others stay for several months.

Because of being raised by humans, integrating a young animal back with its own kind can be difficult. Zoos have developed several techniques for introducing animals to each other. But before the youngster is moved to a permanent home it must be weaned.

WEANING

Weaning is a natural process by which a youngster loses its dependency on mother's milk and starts to eat solid food. In the zoo nursery weaning often happens much sooner than it would if the baby were with its natural mother. The primary reason for weaning zoo babies early is so they can be put back with their own kind as soon as possible.

Solid food is offered to zoo babies as soon as possible.

Eating solid food is a learned skill. When the baby is still young and nursing, it watches its mother while she eats solid food. By watching, the youngster learns which foods are good to eat.

In the zoo nursery, many babies are introduced to the type of food they will be eating as adults long before they are ready to eat solid food. This gives them a chance to play and experiment with the food so that when the weaning process begins, the solid food will be familiar to them.

Weaning is a gradual process that can take weeks or months, depending on the type of animal being weaned. The youngster is offered solid food that is easy for it to eat. For primates this might be in the form of soft fruit or strained baby food. A lion cub might be offered a bowl of meat mixed with its regular milk formula. Hoofed animals are given fresh hay and food pellets like Calf Manna®, which was originally designed to wean dairy calves.

As the young animal eats more solid food, the amount of formula it gets is reduced. When it is eating enough solid food to sustain it, the formula is discontinued, and the weaning process is complete.

BACK TO THE ZOO

Integrating a youngster to its own kind can be tricky and, depending on the type of animal, potentially dangerous. Not all animals are compatible, and because of this the zoo staff is very careful when introducing animals to each other.

Whenever possible keepers try to put the youngster by itself in a cage adjoining the group that it is going to be introduced into. If an adjoining cage is not available, keepers might use what is called a "howdy cage." Howdy cages are made from wire mesh, and are generally used for smaller animals. A howdy cage is essentially a cage within a cage. The youngster is put into the howdy cage, and this is set inside the larger cage. By using these techniques, the animals can see and smell each other without the risk of injury to the animals.

If there have been no problems during this stage of the introduction, the youngster is ready to be tried with the group. Some animals like cats and primates may first be introduced to the group for only short periods of time. Gradually (if things go well) the time that they are with the group is increased until they are spending all of their time in the group.

No matter how the introduction is done, it is closely supervised by the zoo staff. They watch until they are confident that the youngster has successfully been integrated into the group. If there is a problem, the youngster is separated from the others, and the introduction is started again. Eventually, most hand-reared animals are successfully introduced to animals of their own kind.

NATIVE WILDLIFE

Exotic animals are not the only animals that are brought to the zoo nursery to be hand-reared. Many zoo nurseries are asked to take care of orphaned animals found in the local area. Unfortunately, some of these babies would have done fine if they had been left alone in the wild.

Every year dozens of deer fawns are found in forests and meadows by well-meaning people. They pick the fawns up, assuming that they have been abandoned, when in fact the mother is off feeding and will return shortly.

There are times, though, when wild babies are actually orphaned. Mothers are shot, hit by cars, or scared off their nests.

Most of these babies will not be returned to the wild because of the problem of imprinting. Having been raised in the zoo nursery, they lose their fear of humans. In the wild they might approach a hunter, thinking he or she is friendly, and get shot. An animal's best defense in the wild is to stay away from people. This is especially true for mammals that are commonly hunted.

A few babies do get put back in the wild though.

In addition to exotic animals, zoo nurseries are asked to take care of orphaned native animals, like this opossum.

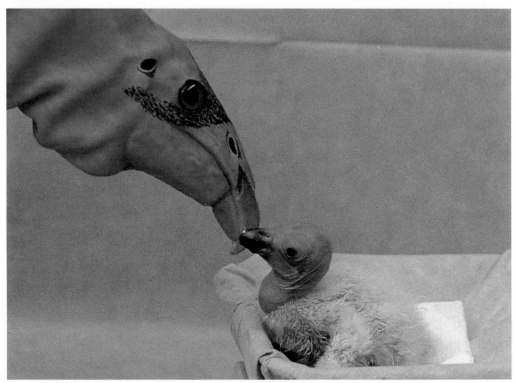

California condor chicks are fed with a puppet to help eliminate the effects of imprinting on humans. Photograph by Mike Wallace, Los Angeles Zoo.

44

Animals that are destined for release to the wild are handled very differently than other zoo nursery babies. To minimize imprinting, they are sometimes fed behind screens, so they cannot see that it is a human feeding them. Some zoo nurseries go so far as to feed wild birds with hand puppets that look like their mothers. The highly endangered California condor is one bird that is usually fed in the zoo nursery with a puppet.

Another technique is to feed the baby in the presence of a mounted adult specimen. If the youngster is a great horned owl chick, a nursery might borrow a mounted adult great horned owl from a natural history museum. The only thing the baby sees when it is fed is the mounted bird, and it imprints on it rather than on people.

BACK TO THE WILD

As soon as the baby is old enough, it is moved to a quiet, isolated enclosure. Human contact is kept to a minimum. The youngster is fed food that it is likely to encounter in the wild. Animals that hunt prey, like owls and hawks, are fed mice. Eventually live food is put into their enclosure and they are allowed to hunt and kill their food. Without this skill they would never survive in the wild.

When they have sharpened their hunting skills, they are ready to be released. A wild release area is chosen in which the animal is commonly found.

Sometimes the animals are taken to the area and simply released. This is called a "hard release." Another technique used is called the "soft release." In a soft release an "acclimation pen" is built at the release site, so the animal can get used to the area. The animal stays in the acclimation pen for several weeks to several months. When the time comes to let it into the wild, the door of the pen is opened and the animal is free to leave when it wants to. Oftentimes, food will be put in the pen several weeks after the animal has left, in case it has trouble finding food on its own.

A chimpanzee baby greets zoo visitors.

Chapter Five

❧ ✦ ❧

INDIVIDUAL
ZOO BABIES

Thousands of exotic animal babies are raised in the zoo nursery every year. Each baby presents its own challenges and joys to the nursery and veterinarian staffs. The following are more examples of animals that for one reason or another have found themselves inside the zoo nursery.

THE CHIMPANZEE

When the chimpanzee came into the nursery she was weak and slightly dehydrated. Her mother had given birth to twins and did not have enough milk to feed both of them. The baby weighed just over three pounds at birth. The nursery staff named her Mary.

The veterinarian examined her and gave her an antibiotic injection to help protect her from disease. A nursery keeper put her in a disposable diaper to keep her clean. After this, she was placed into a human infant incubator with the temperature set at 85 degrees. A soft towel was rolled up and put into the incubator. Mary clung to the towel as if it were her mother.

She was offered three ounces of Similac® eight times a day. Mary was a very willing eater. At first she was fed with a standard baby bottle, but because she ate so quickly, she got air into her stomach. This problem was solved by switching to a Playtex® nurser, which helps stop air getting into the stomach.

Unfortunately there was no other primate in the nursery to play and socialize with Mary. The nursery staff became her playmates. Several times a day they took her from the incubator for play sessions. A large indoor cage with climbing structures was built so that she could exercise. Rules were established for these play sessions. Primates are very intelligent and capable of learning right from wrong. Without rules, a primate can become spoiled and can disrupt the entire nursery operation.

When Mary was old enough, the nursery staff started taking her outside. At first they carried her because she was too young to walk on her own. Eventually they were able to take her for walks around the zoo grounds. On these walks she was able to see other animals and climb trees. When going for walks outside of the nursery compound, keepers used a harness and leash to keep her from straying too far.

When Mary was four months old, cereal was added to her formula. At ten months she was started on solid food. She was offered fruits, vegetables, and Monkey Chow® (a nutritious biscuit especially made for primates). By the time she was fifteen months she was weaned and no longer dependent on formula. She now weighed over fourteen pounds, and was beginning to show signs of

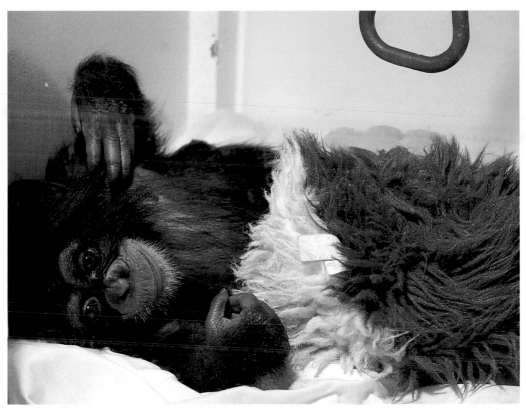

A baby chimpanzee is put in its enclosure for a nap.

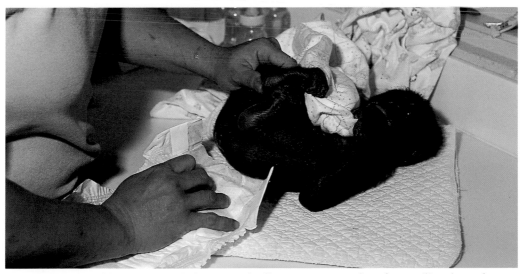

Some primates, like this gorilla baby, are put in diapers to prevent them from soiling themselves.

A chimpanzee plays with a nursery keeper's radio during an outing.

independence. If she didn't want to do something, she learned that she could climb and stay just out of reach of the exasperated nursery staff.

Another zoo called saying that they were looking for a young female chimpanzee to introduce to their group. The nursery staff didn't want to see her go, but they knew it was best. She was shipped to the other zoo and successfully introduced to their group of chimpanzees.

THE CHEETAH CUBS

The keeper concentrated on the closed-circuit television screen. The camera had been set up so he could watch the den box without disturbing the female or her cubs. He hoped this time that Brenda, their eight-year-old cheetah, would raise her cubs successfully. But things did not look good. She had given birth to three cubs the night before, and no one had seen them nurse. The keeper wanted to give her as much time as possible with her cubs. Biologists believe that in some animals, maternal care is a "learned" behavior. If a female is not allowed to practice with cubs, she will not learn how to raise them.

Cheetahs are endangered animals so Brenda's cubs were valuable to the survival of the species. If she didn't take care of the cubs they would have to be taken to the nursery for hand-rearing.

The keeper watched for three more hours. There was no change. Brenda lay several feet from her cubs. If one started to crawl toward her, she moved away. It didn't look as if she was going to care for them.

Closed-circuit television monitors are used to view animals without disturbing them.

The keeper transferred Brenda into the holding area and took the cubs to the nursery. After being examined by the veterinarian, the cubs were put into an infant incubator. One of the three was weaker then the others, and each weighed just under a pound. The veterinarian gave them antibiotic injections to help prevent infection.

They were bottle-fed formula made of one part distilled water to two parts KMR® (Kitten Milk Replacer). KMR® is made for domestic kittens, but works well for exotic cubs.

Within three weeks two of the cubs doubled their weights. But the other cub was having problems. Despite the antibiotic injection, it had caught a respiratory infection. To stop the other cubs from getting the infection, the sick cub was put into an incubator by itself. The veterinarian and nursery staff tried everything they knew to save it, but they were unsuccessful.

A nursery keeper carries two cheetah cubs to their outside exercise area.

The two remaining cubs continued to do well. When they were a month old the nursery staff began to put them into a larger run for exercise. At six weeks they were put there permanently. When the weather was nice, the staff took them outside to play.

At two months they weighed over five pounds each. The staff began to mix their formula with a commercially prepared cat diet made of meat. Gradually the formula in the meat was reduced, and at four months both cubs were totally weaned.

When the cubs were five months old they were separated and sent to different zoos. It was hoped that eventually both of them would produce offspring of their own that would contribute to the dwindling cheetah population.

THE NYALA CALF

The keeper stopped his truck and looked at the herd of nyala through binoculars. Nyala are a type of antelope found in East Africa. The herd was kept in a large paddock of several acres. The keeper carefully scanned the paddock. He was looking for the calf born the day before. Nyala calves are able to follow their mothers soon after they are born. But mothers often lead their newborn calves to the tall grass, where the calf stays hidden except when its mother comes to feed it. After a few days, when the calf is stronger, it joins its mother and the rest of the herd.

The keeper suspected that the calf was being neglected by the mother. He had checked it several times, and each time it was in the exact same spot, and its mother was nowhere near it.

He spotted the calf. It had not moved. Walking into the paddock, he cautiously approached it. The youngster's eyes were closed, and it wasn't moving. He reached down and felt it — the calf was very cold. At first he thought it was dead, but when he picked the frail youngster up it made an almost inaudible sound. He rushed it to the nursery.

At the nursery, the veterinarian and nursery staff worked on the calf for over three hours. Slowly her temperature went up to normal. A tube was gently inserted down the calf's throat into its stomach and it was given a few ounces of cow's colostrum mixed with distilled water. After the feeding, she started to struggle, which meant that she was regaining her strength. She weighed eight pounds, which was small for a female nyala calf. Because of the low weight, the veterinarian suspected that she had been born prematurely. This could account for the mother's neglect. The nursery keepers named her Nadine.

When Nadine was stable she was put into a quiet holding area by herself. A few hours later a nursery keeper tried to feed her a few ounces of cow's colostrum mixed with homogenized whole milk. At first Nadine resisted the nipple, but by gentle coaxing, the keeper was able to get her to take a small amount of formula. Satisfied, the nursery keeper left the holding area to let the calf rest. In an hour the keeper returned and tried again. Nadine took a little more than the first time. The process was repeated throughout the day. When the night keeper came on duty, he joined the nursery keeper to see how she was feeding the calf. He was asked to feed the calf every two hours during his shift.

When the night keeper opened the door for Nadine's last night feed, she stood up, and took a shaky step toward him. During this feeding Nadine eagerly drained the formula from the bottle.

The next morning Nadine was on her feet and looked much stronger. She was fed in the holding area for two more days. When she was strong enough she was put into a larger enclosure with an orphaned muntjac calf and two blackbuck calves. The staff watched them carefully, making sure the youngsters got along.

After a few days the cow's colostrum was discontinued and Nadine was fed whole milk. At two weeks, she was given Calf Manna® and hay. Between

A nyala calf and camel visit over a fence.

bottle feedings Nadine nibbled on the hay and picked at the Calf Manna®. She grew rapidly. At three weeks, Nadine and her penmates were put into a large outdoor pen. By living outdoors they became used to the weather conditions they would encounter as adults.

By the time Nadine was four months old she was eating almost all solid food. Formula was offered only once a day. When she was five months old, the keepers stopped feeding her formula. She was moved to a pen next to the adult nyala yard. For two weeks she interacted with the nyala herd through the fence. When it looked like she would be accepted, she was put in the yard with the others and became an established member of the herd.

THE HARBOR PORPOISE

A very young harbor porpoise calf was found stranded on an Oregon beach. Within hours it was flown to a zoo that had the proper facility to care for it and a staff experienced in rearing stranded marine mammals. On the airplane the baby was kept in a container of ice-cold water. Unlike other mammals, marine mammals tend to overheat and must be kept cool to survive.

When the porpoise arrived at the zoo, the staff was not optimistic about its chances for survival. Baby porpoises are very difficult to hand-rear. Twice before the zoo had received a young stranded harbor porpoise, and both times the calves had died after a few weeks.

The veterinarian examined the baby and said that it appeared to be relatively healthy. The calf was a male. It weighed 25 pounds and was estimated to be a week old.

Replacement milk was made by blending water, herring, Stat® (a high-calorie food supplement), whipping cream, vitamins, and calcium powder.

Porpoise mothers have a unique way of feeding their offspring. The mother contracts her muscles and actually squirts milk into the calf's mouth. Because baby porpoises don't nurse like other mammals, the only way to feed them in captivity is with a stomach tube.

Tubing of the correct diameter was measured and cut to the right length. A large syringe was attached to one end of the tube, and the other end was gently pushed down the calf's throat until it reached the stomach. After the proper amount of formula was poured into the porpoise's stomach through the tube, the tube was gently removed.

The calf was ready to go into the water. The water level of the holding pool was lowered in case the porpoise had trouble swimming. The keepers put on their wet suits. As the porpoise explored its new environment, they stood in the pool and watched. The porpoise calf appeared strong, so the next day the water level was brought up to normal depth.

Within a few days the porpoise was used to being fed with the stomach

The porpoise is weaned onto a diet of whole fish. Photograph by Roland Smith.

tube, and the keepers were able to feed it while it was in the water. They also put floating toys in the water for the porpoise to play with.

The calf gained weight everyday. After three weeks the keepers began to feel that the calf would live. They named the calf Magic.

When Magic had been at the zoo for seven weeks, live fish were put into the pool. To their surprise, Magic caught and ate a few of them. After a few weeks he started to take herring and smelt from the keepers. As the porpoise ate more fish, it became less dependent on formula. At three months, the formula was discontinued.

Because Magic had been hand-reared, his chances of surviving in the wild were slim. It was decided that the best place for him was in the pool with the zoo's other marine mammals.

The zoo had three beluga whales in a large saltwater pool. No one was sure how the belugas would respond to Magic or how Magic would respond to them. The introduction was started by putting Magic in the pool with them for a very short time. At first the belugas chased him around the pool. But Magic was much too fast for them to catch him. As time went by the belugas got used to him. Gradually the time Magic spent in the beluga pool was increased. When it looked like the belugas had accepted him, he was left in the pool permanently.

THE BEST ZOO NURSERY IS
AN EMPTY ZOO NURSERY

Although the zoo nursery is one of the more popular exhibits at the zoo, most zoos would prefer to have no baby animals inside of the zoo nursery. An empty zoo nursery means that the infants born at the zoo are being cared for by their natural mothers.

But for those times when things go wrong for baby animals, it is good to know that they have a place to go and trained professionals to care for them.

INDEX